Dear Parent:
Your child's love of reading starts here!

Every child learns to read in a different way and at his or her own speed. You can help your young reader improve and become more confident by encouraging his or her own interests and abilities. You can also guide your child's spiritual development by reading stories with biblical values and Bible stories, like I Can Read! books published by Zonderkidz. From books your child reads with you to the first books he or she reads alone, there are I Can Read! books for every stage of reading:

SHARED READING
Basic language, word repetition, and whimsical illustrations, ideal for sharing with your emergent reader.

BEGINNING READING
Short sentences, familiar words, and simple concepts for children eager to read on their own.

READING WITH HELP
Engaging stories, longer sentences, and language play for developing readers.

READING ALONE
Complex plots, challenging vocabulary, and high-interest topics for the independent reader.

ADVANCED READING
Short paragraphs, chapters, and exciting themes for the perfect bridge to chapter books.

I Can Read! books have introduced children to the joy of reading since 1957. Featuring award-winning authors and illustrators and a fabulous cast of beloved characters, I Can Read! books set the standard for beginning readers.

A lifetime of discovery begins with the magical words **"I Can Read!"**

Visit www.icanread.com for information on enriching your child's reading experience.
Visit www.zonderkidz.com for more Zonderkidz I Can Read! titles.

"My God sent his angel. And his angel shut the mouths of the lions. They haven't hurt me at all."
—Daniel 6:22

ZONDERKIDZ

Daniel and the Lions
Copyright © 2008 by Mission City Press. All Rights Reserved. All Beginner's Bible copyrights and trademarks (including art, text, characters, etc.) are owned by Mission City Press and licensed by Zondervan of Grand Rapids, Michigan.

Requests for information should be addressed to:

Zonderkidz, *Grand Rapids, Michigan 49530*

Library of Congress Cataloging-in-Publication Data

Daniel and the lions : my first I can read! / illustrated by Kelly Pulley
    p.   cm. — (I can read)
  ISBN 978-0-310-71551-1 (softcover : alk. paper)
  1. Daniel (Biblical figure)—Juvenile literature. 2. Bible stories, English—O.T.
Daniel. I. Pulley, Kelly, ill.
BS580.D2D367 2008
224'.509505—dc22   2007012120

Editor: Kristen Tuinstra
Art direction: Jody Langley
Cover design: Sarah Molegraaf

Printed in the United States of America

16 17 18 /WOR/ 20 19 18 17

I Can Read!

My First — SHARED READING

The Beginner's Bible

Daniel and the Lions

pictures by Kelly Pulley

Daniel was a good man.

He loved God very much.

Daniel went to the king.

The king loved Daniel.

Daniel helped the king.

Because he loved God, some
men did not like Daniel.
The men made an evil plan.

The men went to the king.
"King, you are a great man,"
they said.

"People should pray
only to you."

The men said, "If they do not,
we will put them
in the lions' den."

The men wanted to get Daniel
in big trouble.

The king said, "Okay."
He did not know it was a
trap for Daniel.

Daniel prayed only to God.

The men saw Daniel praying.
He did not stop praying to God.

The men told the king
about Daniel.

"King, your helper Daniel
does not obey your rule,"
the men said.

"Daniel was praying
to God. Not to you."

The men had tricked the king.

Guards came to take
Daniel away to the
lions' den.

The king shook his head.
The rule said pray only to
the king.

But Daniel would not stop.

He would pray only to God.

The king did not
want to hurt Daniel.

The king said, "Daniel, I hope your God will save you."

Daniel was thrown into the
lions' den.

The king was very sad.

Daniel prayed to God.
He asked God to watch
over him.

So God sent his angel
to help Daniel.
Daniel was safe all night.

In the morning,
the king woke up.
He ran to see Daniel.

The king called, "Daniel,
are you okay?
Did your God save you?"

"Yes," said Daniel.
"God's angel helped me
with the lions!"

The king was so happy!
"Come with me, Daniel."

The king told all his people,
"Daniel's God is great!
Let us pray only to God."